The Life of an Ordinary Man

By Duane Anderson

Cyberwit.net
HIG 45 Kaushambi Kunj, Kalindipuram
Allahabad - 211011 (U.P.) India
http://www.cyberwit.net
Tel: +(91) 9415091004
E-mail: info@cyberwit.net

Printed at Repro India Limited.

Acknowledgements

Thanks are due to the following periodicals in whose pages these poems first appeared.

Publication	**Poem**
Academy of the Heart and Mind	"The Secret of Deep Sleep;" "Just for You"
Adelaide Literary Magazine	"My First Pet;" "The Paper Trail"
Cholla Needles	"Accidental Meeting;" "I Have Been Told That I Am Alive;" "Ugly vs. Ugly;" "What Can I Say?;" "A Very Slow Day;" "Some Days Are Sunny;" "Mother Did This to Me;" "Wind Senses;" "Pepe le Pew;" "Deliberation;" "Persistence Pays Off;" "The Unknown Celebrity;" "One of Life's Mysteries;" "Maybe Tomorrow Will Be the Right Day;" "Sunburn, Cruel Sun;" "Beauty Rest;" "Good Memories Day;" "Arrowheads;" "Justice;" "The Uninvited Passenger;" "Keeping the Yawns to a Minimum;" "Handicap Parking;" "A Life in Limbo;" "The Ant and Its Shadow"
Down in the Dirt	"Oh Wise One;" "Current Occupant;" "Philosophy 101"
Evening Street Review	"Mr. Regular"
Fictional Café	Estate "Planning Offer;" "New Morning Ritual;" "A Look Back;" "Hokey Pokey;" "The Hill Up Ahead"

Flora Fiction	"St. Stanislaus Festival"
Gas: Poetry, Art and Music	"The Shoe Enthusiast "
Grey Sparrow Journal	"An Eye Exam for Mr. Magoo"
Hidden Peak Press	"Jigsaw Puzzle"
Home Planet News	"Road Construction;" "Clown Sporting Shoes"
Journal of Expressive Writing	"Mirror Freedom"
Knot Magazine	"Good Deed;" "Preferred Walking Style;" "Manual Toothbrush"
Modern Literature	"Train Crossing"
North Dakota Quarterly	"Breaking the Rules "
Nuthouse Magazine	"Talking Shoes;" "Let Me Help You"
October Hill	"That's Life"
Open Door Poetry Magazine	"Clouds: The Endless Movie:" "Goodbye to a Memory;" "Tornado Season;" "Let Me Sleep;" "Just Tell Me the Truth, What's Bothering You?"
Our Poetry Archive	"Another Day of Life;" "Yet Another Choice in Life;" "Graffiti;" "Forty-One Steps;" "The Pacifist"
Scarlet Leaf Review	"Discount Department Store Shopping"
Taj Mahal	"Morning Workout"
The Amazine	"Hitting the Jackpot"
The Good Men Project	"Life Cycle Changes"

Torrid Literature Journal   "A Choice of Paths"

W-Poesis   "Our Paths Crossed"

International Poets Anthology (Edited by Sourav Sarkar) (Cooch Behar Books)   "The Unknown Flower"

Winter (Edited by Sourav Sarkar) (Cooch Behar Books)

"Winter Blues"

Winter Splinter Anthology (Edited by William Mays) Mays Publishing

"Unfriendly Winter Welcome"

Contents

I Have Been Told That I Am Alive

I have been told that I am alive,
but then, I'm not so sure.
Maybe it is a life not worth living
as I do not finish first in anything I do.

Not first in gross income,
nor the poorest,
not first in being the fattest man on earth,
nor the skinniest,

not the tallest,
nor the shortest,
not the most handsome,
nor the ugliest man on earth.

I am average,
and what is so special about that,
though there are a few that love me
and a few that I love back.,

so I guess that should mean something.
Maybe I am alive after all
like I have been told.
Time will tell.

Accidental Meeting

The sign at the auto collision center stated,
'We would love to meet you by accident.'
I'm sure they would, but if I had a choice,
I rather they didn't, no offense taken,

but they got their wish anyway, getting into an accident,
my insurance company totaling the car,
but that no longer mattered since I was in heaven
after spending some time in hell during that fatal crash.

You can still meet me if you want,
but it will have to be at my funeral,
but forgive me if I do not say hello,
I do not want to scare you, being that I am no longer alive,

but I hope I am smiling as I lay in my casket,
not wanting anyone to see me being sad one last time.
And as for my car, I left it to you in my will.
Do with it as you wish, my final gift to you.

Ugly vs. Ugly

I called my brother, and told him
his good-looking brother was calling him,
but he disagreed with me, saying

it was the ugly one who was calling him,
a longstanding issue neither of us could agree on,
both greeting each other with 'Hi Ugly.'

It was a name we both had in common,
but when I looked into the mirror,
I only saw beauty.

I would never understand what my brother
was talking about, he must have become blind
was all I could come up with.

What Can I Say?

What did I miss
as I dozed off into another world,
a solar eclipse,
an astronaut landing on the moon,
a fly landing on my nose,
a stampede of elephants
running through the house,
Publishers Clearing House sweepstakes
ringing my doorbell,
a parade on my street,
a three-ring circus in my living room?
I would never know,
I did not wake up,
but if I had to guess,
it would have been a symphony of snores,
and I missed it once again. Oh darn!

A Very Slow Day

I watched a cicada
resting on the deck,
it did not move,

then watched a rabbit
munching on the grass
for its evening meal,

while I sat on the deck
watching what was going on
in the neighborhood.

Some for leisure,
some for survival,
and one of boredom.

Some Days Are Sunny

The sign in the sandwich shop said
'Not every day is a sunny day,
some days you're the pigeon,
some days you're the statue.'

Today was my sunny day,
my special day,
and I was the pigeon,
so watch out statue,

run and hide if you can
for I will be out to celebrate,
and what may fall,
will find a place to land.

Train Crossing

Lit up across the Interstate,
the video board message stated
'Look, listen, and live.
Watch out at railroad crossings.'

I thought it a strange bulletin,
for in all my years traveling the Interstate,
I had yet to see a train crossing,
nor were there any train crossing signs,

stop signs, or even a traffic light.
Yes, there were plenty of orange cones
and road construction signs, but maintenance
was preferred over pot holes in the road.

The only signs found were for deer crossings,
but no deer were currently in sight.
Maybe later on, in the middle of night,
there would be a train of deer crossing the road,

the first deer wearing an engineer's hat,
and the last one, carrying a flashing a red lamp.
Clickity clack, clickity clack,
watch out for the deer train running down the tracks.

Clouds: The Endless Movie

Clouds overhead,
floating by,
dressed all in white,
highlighted by a blue-sky.

They are the movie of the day
as they slowly pass by.
I keep watching,
not wanting to miss the ending

when the sky becomes too dark
and disappears into night,
waiting for a second viewing
as I replay them in my dreams.

Mother Did This to Me

Mother Nature,
we've had our disputes
from time to time,
and today, was one of those special days.
You said "Let there be ice,"
and there it was, sneaking up on me,
in a cloud of freezing fog,
and me, thinking the pavement was only wet.
Down I went, out for the count,
blood on the sidewalk, blood on my clothes,
now walking around
with one black eye and four stitches.
Yes, Mother Nature,
you did well with your disguise, for you
always said that you played no favorites,
doing it one more time, not even letting
the very last day of the year go to waste,
always keeping current with your bag of tricks.
I should have paid attention to your past deeds,
instead of complaining like I did, knowing
your knockout punch could have been worst,
but now, I think you owe me, a debt
I know I will never be able to collect.

The Shoe Enthusiast

The only mail from today's delivery,
a flyer addressed to my wife,
or the current shoe enthusiast,
adding the second addressee
as a precaution in case we had moved
and did not provide a forwarding address,
hoping one of the new owners

would also be a shoe aficionado, though I never
realized my wife was one of the chosen ones,
though she did have many more shoes than I,
knowing I could never be called one of the special ones,
for I waited until one of my shoes became fatigued,
with worn-out souls and heels, cracked sides,
scuffed up beyond any help from a shoe shine.

It had to be out of necessity before I ever
visited a shoe store on purpose.
My feet, had they grown, or shrunk,
had I met death before new shoes were required?
There was no need for an extra pair sitting around
like the spare tire for a car,
just waiting for a blowout.

Talking Shoes

Her shoes were a constant reminder
whenever she walked, squeaking,
talking to her with each step, whether
it was walking on carpets or hardwood floors,
or if the bottoms were wet or dry,
unless she was willing to give them a rest.

Shoes, constant complainers,
ones, not meant for walking,
as my tortured ears were forced to listen to
each word as I walked along by her side.
Shoes, ready for retirement,
long before taking their first steps after birth.

To other wearers,
their history would have been short,
immediately donated to some charity
so they could nag someone else,
as most wearers preferred shoes that
knew the skills of mime.

Wind Senses

I cannot see the wind,
not that I am blind, but it is invisible to my eyes.
I only see what the wind does to the trees,
moving its branches back and forth, at times,
knocking the weaker ones to the ground,

and does the wind taste sweet like a candy bar,
or sour like a lime,
and does it stink like a skunk,
or inviting like a bubble bath?
I do not know; for I can neither taste or smell it.

The wind only arouses two of my remaining senses.
I feel it as it moves,
making it hard to walk when meeting it face to face,
and when following in its path,
let me flap my wings, I feel as if I could fly,

and I hear the wind
as it howls in my ears
and flexes its large muscles,
always knowing when it is at its strongest,
moving so quickly across the landscape.

Two senses present,
three senses absent,
and my desire to visit it at the moment,
I am leaning on passing for the time being,
it is traveling at a faster speed than I prefer.

Pepé Le Pew

My wife walked into the family room
where I had taken root for the evening,
me, sitting in my favorite recliner,

relaxing, watching television,
then she quickly went into the kitchen,
lighting a scented candle,

her quiet way of saying something stunk,
though we did not cook anything
in the kitchen that evening,

and the garbage had already been taken
out for the night,
leaving me with only one conclusion,

that I was the one, and needed shower
even after having taken one earlier that morning.
Pepé Le Pew, that must be me.

Deliberation

At times, I wonder if it was all worth it,
getting a knee replaced through surgery.
It wasn't like it was an easy switch,
pulling the old one out,
placing the new one in,
like replacing batteries in a flashlight.

Now, the leg, swollen up like a balloon,
muscles all tight,
the leg and foot, black and blue,
I sit in the house day after day working
on the exercises assigned by a physical therapist
as if I had gone back to school after a long hiatus.

It is a new subject that I am still getting used to,
but I do my homework several times a day
wanting to return to normal as quickly as possible,
but at the same time wondering if it was all worth it.
The jury is in deliberation,
and I will have to wait to see if justice will prevail.

Let Me Help You

On the local news today,
the newscaster said a body
was found floating in the river,
and to call a special number

if anyone knew anything about it
to help the local law officials out,
but the only thing I could tell them
was that they could eliminate me

as the potential victim.
I was still alive and nowhere near the river,
hoping this helped them out in this case,
one always eager to offer a helping hand.

Life Cycle Changes

Two grandsons, reaching that age
when they no longer wanted to take naps,
and grandfather, reaching that stage
when he needed them once again.

Two, packed full of energy,
batteries totally charged,
and the other one, running on empty,
his batteries in need of a revitalization.

The grandsons, ready to stop their siestas
having reached the next stage of development,
and the grandfather, ready to be reintroduced
to an old tradition of his past.

Changes in the life cycle, no longer
calling it a nap, but resting his eyes,
something now required several times a day
as he regenerated on a recliner or couch.

A lifesaving event for grandpa,
taking in these special moments
as the Energizer Bunny continues
to jump him back to life each day.

Oh Wise One

They asked what my name was
so they didn't have to refer me as just Guy,
and I replied, call me Wise One.
After all, there were still a few of us left in the world,
otherwise, I may not get another chance
to let them know how important
I was to the world according to my own mind,

so please take note, give me the respect that I deserve.
If you want any of my other aliases,
you can call me The Thinker, Scholar, Prophet,
and I could go on and on with all of my other names,
but by now, you know of my significance,
and you can thank me by knowing
I am honoring you with my presence.

Current Occupant

Yes, Current Occupant
was one of the aliases I was known to have used,
that, along with John Smith,

Hey You, and Ugly Man,
among a few others,
but today, I was glad just to get something

in the mail addressed to one of them,
making me feel important for a moment,
bringing me peace of mind.

Now that I know I have finally been found,
I am hoping for another piece in tomorrow's mail
to continue my new sense of fandom.

Persistence Pays Off

My phone rang,
only to hear a recorded message
stating my social security number
had been suspended, and if I wanted
to find out more of the details,
to punch 1. Instead, I hung up,

jumping up and down in delight.
Did it mean I no longer existed,
and no longer had to pay taxes to the IRS,
a free man, a man with no identity?
Two more calls followed,
different phone numbers, but the same message.

I give up, I give up, I tell them.
Here is my social security number.
It is 111-22-3333,
a number I no longer need.
Have fun with it,
as I disappear into obscurity.

The Unknown Celebrity

I am a celebrity, of sorts. I made it
on the local TV news a few times in my life,
once filmed taking my Christmas tree
off the roof of my car at a recycling site,

another being interviewed
after donating at a blood drive,
and then there was the commercial I was in
as one of the extras standing in the background,

and don't forget the time I was accepted to
be an extra in a movie to be filmed
at our church, only four days later
to be told I wasn't needed afterwards.

You may not have heard of me,
but I am around if you catch me at the right moment,
just don't expect to find me on the society pages,
not quite yet anyway.

One of Life's Mysteries

Do you remember why you showed
up at my doorstep?

Was it to sell me a something,
something I really needed,

inform me of a political candidate
that you wanted me to vote for,

deliver a package that was delivered
to your house by mistake,

give me a tomato from your garden,
one too many for your needs,

tell me the meaning of life,
or just to see my smiling face?

My door is open,
let me know what it is that I am waiting for?

Maybe Tomorrow Will Be the Right Day

I wanted to go for a walk,
but I didn't want to fight the strong winds
that were blowing around outside.

I wanted to got something to eat,
but I didn't want to get out of my chair
and head to the refrigerator.

I wanted to read a book,
but my library was downstairs
and I didn't feel like going down the stairs.

I said I wanted to do various things,
but I guess it wasn't the right day
to get them done.

Maybe tomorrow will be the right day.

Sunburn, Cruel Sun

I got sunburned on the top of my head today.
Did that make me a redhead,
or a redskin?

Blame it on a loss of hair,
blame it on the sun,
blame it on an idiot outside
in the sun without a hat,
blame it on all of the above,

but I ruled out answers three and four
as potential possibilities,
and chose answer number two,
blaming it on the sun,
a sun that had no mercy on me.

Beauty Rest

He said he was ready to go to bed
and get a little beauty rest,
but he woke up the same as the day before,
the ugliest man in the world.

Maybe he felt better looking,
and that was all that mattered.
Maybe the beauty went to someone else,
but I know it wasn't me, I didn't need it.

Being brothers, there was little chance
of him improving his looks over me
other than wearing a mask or paper bag,
but now that I look back at it,

he was wearing a paper bag over his head
as he walked out of the bedroom into the kitchen.
Who knew,
a miracle after all.

Good Memories Day

Today was June twelfth,
the sixth month, and twelfth day of the year,
numbers six and twelve,
or run them altogether, 612,
the house number where I lived
for over twenty years of my life,
then another forty years of visiting
my parents after moving away.

June twelfth, a day to remember
all the good things that happened in that house,
celebrating birthdays, sharing meals together,
playing games, learning a few of life's lessons,
a part of my history,
and now, a personal holiday,
like the Fourth of July and Christmas.
I call it Good Memories Day.

Goodbye to a Memory

Once again, I found myself
dining at a Mexican restaurant,
one I had fond memories of,

ordering the same food and drinks
I remembered having
on my prior visit years ago,

but maybe my tastes had changed,
or they had a new chef
and had changed their recipes,

or, just maybe, I had one too many margaritas
my last time around, corrupting the old memory bank,
but now, plans on returning again

were at the point of no return,
any good memories having already
faded into a deep, dark, black hole.

Estate Planning Offers

It was confirmed I was getting older after
receiving an email on an estate planning webinar
addressed to the Class of 1975,
and then sending it right during the coronavirus pandemic,

to a group that I was a part of,
the higher at-risk age group.
Was it bad timing or a coincidence,
but hoped their message found me

and my loved ones healthy and well.
As for my estate planning,
I leave you all my old college yearbooks,
including a few pictures to remember me by,

my diploma, stating I graduated from your college,
something you remind me of from time to time,
along with my heartfelt gratitude, but other than this,
thanks for the offer, but I will take a pass at this time.

The Secret of Deep Sleep

I was tired and ready for some sleep.
I turned on the television, looking for something
boring, a station carrying baseball.

It didn't matter what teams were playing,
what their win/loss records were.
Baseball hypnotized me into a deep slumber,

and hoped it was for a double header, but I
needed the rest and would take whatever I could get,
managing a full nine innings of sleep.

No hits, no walks, no runs,
nothing but deep snores
and a peaceful sleep.

New Morning Ritual

In days of old, it used to be called a newspaper,
but now it is more like a newsletter,
short, condensed,
a Cliff Notes version of its former self

giving me a sense of what was going on,
but still, it just wasn't the same.
My morning ritual had gotten shortened,
and I was still trying to figure out

how to fill that gap in my daily schedule,
maybe having to hit the snooze button on the alarm
clock one more time before getting out of bed
and welcoming in morning.

Hitting the Jackpot

The birds were used to
the stupid things that I did,
and today, they got their money's worth.
They looked,
they smiled,
they laughed
as they watched from the fence railing
while I sat lounging on the deck chair,
fast asleep,
getting a secret sunburn.
Today was a bonus day,
never wanting to disappoint my fans.

A Look Back

Look at the past,
look at the present.
My before
and after pictures,

one in my teens,
head full of hair,
one in my sixties,
head full of nothing.

Where were all the things learned
from all the years in between,
but time took hold
and all was forgotten

Look at one,
full of potential,
then look at the other,
head turned around to see what happened.

Arrowheads

I looked at the box of Indian arrowheads
sitting in the dresser drawer,
two of them handed down to me by my grandfather
sixty years ago, and a third one, found

near a creek when I was a young boy.
I remember taking the arrowheads
to school for show and tell,
items I was proud to show off,

and now, I wished to go back in time,
to the time when my grandfather
first handed the arrowheads to me,
to once again hear what he told me on

how he came in possession of them,
then back further in time
to when the Indians made the arrowheads,
fired the arrow from the bow for its last time,

wondering what it was aimed at, and if it hit its mark?
The arrowheads future, to be passed down
to my grandchildren, hoping they too
will be honored in having a part of history.

Another Day of Life

I noticed my name listed
in the morning paper's obituary,
and asked if it was really me?
The name had a familiar ring to it,
though the picture looked nothing like me.

I finally decided I was still alive
and went out to celebrate,
not to eulogize someone else's death,
but observe and honor another day of life, knowing
being alive was much better than the alternative.

That's Life

I bumped into my chair
as I walked past it, and said 'Ouch,'
even though there was no pain.

I sounded like I was looking for sympathy,
but no one was around to hear me,
or feel the pain that was not there.

I may have to do something more senseless
before I feel the pain. That moment will surely come.
It is only a matter of time.

Just for You

Just for you,
it snowed on your birthday
in order to give you something to do,
and knowing Mother Nature,
she didn't skimp,
leaving you with plenty of snow,
even an extra helping,
so go out into the snow,
have fun, shovel your sidewalk,
throw snowballs, go sledding, complain.
It's your day, the choice is all yours.

Tornado Season

Today was the best time for a tornado
to sneak up and surprise everyone,
at ten in the morning,
the first Saturday of the month
when the sirens were tested,
and most ignored their warnings,
knowing they were set to go off.
Yes, tornado, sneak up.
No one will know until it is too late,
except for one person, me, the worry wart,
who will be down in his bunker,
the only one waiting for a surprise attack.

Philosophy 101

I wasn't a professor of philosophy.
I didn't teach Spinoza, Descartes, Aristotle,
or even Kinky Friedman,
but I had my own kind of philosophy
that I preached and followed.
If you don't want to tread water
the rest of your life, get out of the water.
Don't kick the wall
unless you want to break a few toes.
Don't look at yourself in a mirror
if you want to see beauty.
If you smell like a skunk,
you may want to change colognes.
If you enjoy having company, don't forget
to welcome the cockroaches into your home.
Take a walk around the block,
see a small part of the world,
or listen to my words,
you may learn something yet.

Mr. Regular

Every Monday, I went to the same
grocery store to purchase some fresh salmon
to be cooked for that night's meal.
Though the salmon may be marinated
and cooked differently each week,
one thing was common,
I showed up each Monday, me, Mr. Regular,
and the butchers behind the meat counter
all knew what I was there for as soon as
I blessed them with my presence.

One salmon piece, they would ask,
knowing fully well that was the case,
then thanked me for my order,
and asked if I needed anything else.
They may not have known my name,
but I wondered if they had a nick name
of the their own for me?
Was it Salmon Man, or Fish Face, or something else?
I am sure one existed,
but maybe it was best it was left unknown by me.

Unfriendly Winter Welcome

Cars and trucks lie in ditches,
now abandoned, buried in snow,
wrapped with yellow tape.
The state patrol has marked
 the cars and trucks to be towed away
in the days to come.
After awhile,
I lose count of the number of
abandoned vehicles.

Up ahead,
a crash has occurred.
The left lane is closed,
traffic slowing to a crawl,
snow still falling,
and accumulating on the interstate.
We pass the accident,
three state patrol cars,
one tow truck,
and one car still remaining from the accident.

As we continue our travel,
we maintain a slower speed,
making it safely to our destination,
wanting no part of visiting
a car repair shop or hospital.

St. Stanislaus Festival

Tell me why I was standing in line holding
an umbrella during a downpour, for I really
didn't have a sane reason? Yes, the line

was a little shorter than the year before,
but still, it didn't make me feel any better
as I stood in a food line with hundreds

of others just like me, getting wet,
some holding umbrellas, some wearing rain
ponchos, while others with no extra protection

from the rain other than the clothes on their
backs that they were wearing.
There was no line at the ticket booth

for those wishing to purchase tickets
for any of the carnival rides, and besides,
only one carnival ride was in action,

the Ferris Wheel, and it had only one rider
braving the rain. All the other carnival workers
were sitting inside some of the dragons

from the Dizzy Dragon ride, not
wanting to get any wetter than they
already were. I stood in line for an hour

waiting to get my annual dosage of Polish foods
consisting of two of my favorites, Golabkis and Peroiges,
something my system tells me I need once a year.

I must have been crazy for standing in line
in the rain for an hour, so tomorrow,
I am making an appointment to see a psychiatrist.

The Unknown Flower

The cloth flowers in our living room
are always in bloom.
They do not require water,
nor do they wither away
like the rest of life.
Yes, they gather dust
and maybe my wife
will get bored with them
and replace them with some other
type of flower and color
and then they too will be buried,
but not in a cemetery,
but in a dump
where the only visitors
are the garbage trucks
there to dump more trash on top of them.
There will be on one to place
flowers on top its grave.
No one will remember that it is there.
There will be no tombstone
with its name
or date of birth and death
because it was given no name
and no one kept track
of when it was created
or when it was placed in the trash.
It will always be the unknown flowers
and will be forgotten,
even by me.

Good Deed

On my early morning walk I passed by
the Walmart parking lot, and as usual
there were plenty of cars in the lot even
though it was only 5:30 in the morning.
Some might have been shopping after getting

off work before heading home while others may have
needed something before they headed off to work.
I was doing neither. I was just on my early
morning walk, my daily ritual when it
wasn't raining or too terribly cold outside,

and today I noticed the dimmer lights still on
one of the cars in the lot, but I figured it was
just one of the employees who had recently arrived
since the car was on the back side of the lot,
the furthest away from the front doors.

I continued my walk for another two blocks
then returned to go back home.
The car's dimmer lights were still on,
but I could not see anyone in the front seat
until getting within a few feet of the car finding

that it was still running, and the once upon time
driver was fast asleep in the fully reclined front seat.
I had planned on doing a good deed by
getting the make and license number of the car
to report it to someone working inside

the store to advise that one of their employees'
car lights were still on, but I no longer needed
to do that since that person was still in the car,
but still, I did my good deed anyway, by not waking
him up, letting Sleeping Beauty continue to sleep in peace.

Preferred Walking Style

He was walking on the sidewalk along the
busy street wearing pants and a short sleeve shirt,
holding an umbrella propped open,
though it wasn't raining at the time and there
wasn't any hint of rain from looking at the sky,

and rain was not in the forecast for the day.
The sun was out with no clouds
for it to hide behind and the temperature
was comfortable, only in the low eighties.
Covering up with an umbrella

was one method of avoiding getting
sunburned by not allowing the sunshine to
land on his skin denying him of his daily dose
of Vitamin D, but what could I say, I was
in my car as I drove by him, the windows

rolled up with the air conditioner turned on,
other than if I had been walking I would
have worn shorts and a T-shirt along with
a baseball cap to protect my balding head.

Each of us has our own preferred
method of walking on a sunny day,
but I prefer not holding anything in my hands,
other than maybe an ice cream cone
as I stroll along on a nice summer afternoon.

Manual Toothbrush

In today's Sunday paper there was a
manufacturer's coupon for a toothbrush,
but it said it was for a manual toothbrush,

not knowing why it just couldn't be
listed as a toothbrush and would be
differentiated by calling the other kind

an electric toothbrush, though that
probably isn't really true either?
It is really a battery powered toothbrush

since they aren't attached to any power cords,
and not knowing if anything such thing
existed as a solar power toothbrush

or a wind power toothbrush.
Did they call other items with the manual
label, for example, like manual hammers,

though I now had a pounding headache
from the woodpecker hammering away on the
tree outside my window, or a manual screwdriver,

though I preferred the kind of screwdriver
prepared with orange juice and vodka,
or a manual chair,

though I doubt I would care for the electric chair
unless if I were in a prison and
didn't quite care for my new lodgings?

Did the coupon really need the adjective of manual
to further describe it for the one-dollar discount
when used at the store to purchase the toothbrush?

Our Paths Crossed

Our paths crossed,
I said hi, he said nothing.
We were both taking a walk,
me for exercise,
him, maybe his mode of transportation.
I was not trying to be friends,
nor trying to be enemies,
but it wasn't like he didn't see me,
for he carried no white cane
nor held the leash of any seeing eye dog.
There wasn't anyone else around,

and I wasn't trying to be invisible.
Was it wrong to say hi or good evening?
We each had our reasons for walking,
getting to where we wanted to go.
After my small attempt at humanity,
we both kept on walking,
I going east, he going west.
I had never seen him before, and it
was not likely I would ever see him again.
At times, the paths of two people will cross,
and still, remain strangers, forever.

Justice

She sat in her car, a car she
could not get to move, forward or
backward, though there was nothing
mechanically wrong with the car.

She had made a U-turn
at a point in the road clearly
marked with a No U-Turn sign,
driving over a curb,

only to get high centered.
The dirt, once along the curb,
worn into a deep rut by
who knows how many vehicles before

had made this same U-turn as she.
I smiled and gave her a thumbs up
as I passed by her, knowing that justice
had finally been served.

Discount Department Store Shopping

The clerk asked me if I was finding everything
alright as I pushed my cart down the aisle of a
large discount department store even though

my shopping cart was completely empty.
I guess everything was going just right
if it was my way of getting in my morning walk,

pushing an empty cart up and down the aisles,
or if I was a magician and had caused the items
I was going to purchase to magically disappear,

but I had just started my shopping and had yet to reach
the area where I hoped to find the items I was looking for,
which to my dismay, found they were all out of on this trip,

but instead of going home right away,
I thought, oh what the hell, I might as well get
some benefit from my futile effort and

decided to get my morning walk in after all,
since it was sixty degrees warmer inside the store
than it was outside in the frigid winter wonderland.

Winter Blues

It was six degrees below zero when the furnace
went out, the thermostat showing the temperature
inside was now down to fifty degrees,

and slowly getting colder when she asked
"Can you tell me why this happens on the coldest
day of the year?", but wait I say, it's still early in the

season and could get a hell of lot colder, so today
just might not end up being the coldest day of the year,
and yes, it could have also come at a worse time,

maybe if she had gone on a Caribbean cruise
or on a visit to see Mickey Mouse at Disney World
when the furnace stopped running and no one

would be home for days with the temperature
slowly decreasing to below freezing as the water
pipes froze, bursting, causing water to flow all over

the house, and what did she expect, for the furnace to
fail during the summer when it wasn't even turned on?
Yes, it may not be pleasant, but this was one of the

outcomes that I thought of as I sipped on another Pina
Colada, laying on a hammock on a sandy beach in Hawaii.
Winter blues, each to our own choosing.

Let Me Sleep

If I fall asleep watching the movie,
it only means my sleep has more importance
than what is on the screen,
no matter how many millions it cost to film it,
or how many favorable reviews it received.
Let me sleep.

My sleep is well worth the price
of the movie ticket, knowing my dreams
will more than make up for its cost,
and if I fall asleep when I am at work,
fire my ass,
my sleep is well worth the price.

Sleep, a precious commodity,
and a scarcity at night,
most welcomed with open arms when it comes,
no matter how steep the cost,
the movies I may have missed,
the jobs I may have lost.

Don't wake me up,
just let me sleep.
My dreams will keep me contented.

Breaking the Rules

The poetry reading was held at the library,
where on the ends of the bookshelves,
signs were posted stating no smoking, food, or drink,
but then, right next to the area where the reading was being
held, were refreshments of lemonade, water, and cookies.

I figured by not breaking all three of the rules
it would probably be okay, so I had some water and a cookie.
If they were going to offer everyone refreshments,
I wasn't going to be one to turn them down,
no matter what the sign said.

If they had also offered cigarettes and cigars,
I would have declined that offer for
there were some things I could live without.
Some signs were just meant to be ignored,
especially if they provided the forbidden items to all who came,

and that evening, there was one other rule being broken,
that of being quiet as a mime in a library,
something the poets ignored as they read their poems out loud,
and I was glad no one was shushing them
as they read their poems to everyone's enjoyment.

The Uninvited Passenger

As I got into my car, I found it impossible
not to notice the fly resting on the hood,
it's face reminding me of my younger brother.

I assumed it would fly away as soon as
I started the car and went on my way,
but it stayed put, like it was stuck on flypaper,

and no matter how hard it tried,
it couldn't get off the hood of the car.
Even as I sped up, its legs remained in place,

seemingly having no desire to leave,
and figured by then, it must have liked me
after our short time spent together,

even though we hadn't properly been introduced,
and wondered if it wanted to go home with me
to meet the rest of my family,

as I had no clue as to its intentions.
It wasn't that I was driving a taxi, looking for a fare,
and even if I were, it didn't look to have any

credit cards or cash to pay me for the ride,
wondering if it was tired of its old neighborhood,
ready for someplace new,

too tired to pilot there itself,
knowing the car was a much faster option,
Finally, after travelling several miles along on my route home,

it took off as I came to a stop at a traffic light,
but as it left, I felt the least it could have done
was thanked me for the free ride.

Yet Another Choice in Life

All I wanted to do was go to the store to find
an insecticide to kill some ants that had been
congregating by the front door of the house.

Little did I know I would have so many choices,
lemon scent, orange scent, lavender scent,
and not to be undone, an outdoor fresh scent,

and even with so many choices, I was not tempted
to smell each one as some might do when checking
out which perfume or cologne to purchase,

because somehow, I didn't quite think it would
be beneficial for my health to smell the fumes for
something that was meant to kill ants and roaches,

and I very much doubted if the ants would care
which scent I used, so from the four fragrances,
I chose the outdoor fresh scent which

seemed something to best to blend in
with the scent already outdoors.
As for the ants, I would tell them goodbye,

so long, as I sprayed the territory they had invaded,
and maybe say a little prayer
as I bury them in a mass grave in the backyard.

Graffiti

The graffiti artist wrote 'Wash Me'
on the rear window of a car
completely covered by dust,
using only their finger instead of the usual tools
of the trade, that of a handy can of spray paint,
and I wondered if the car owner called
the police to file a report about the graffiti,
and if the police took any finger prints
from the car to help them identify the felon
if it was truly being considered as a crime,
or instead, just laughing it off, as they wrote
him up for reporting a bogus crime
advising him what he probably should
have done in the first place, by just
washing his car to remove those words?
In the end, the car remained unwashed,
leaving the words in place, after all,
it seemed to be who he was,
one to do nothing.

Forty-One Steps

They moved into an apartment,
and were given three options to choose from,
something on the first floor
with no steps to maneuver,
or the second floor with only
twenty-one steps to walk up,
but there was also a third option,
the one that they chose,
the third floor with forty-one steps.
It had the maximum number of steps
for the apartment complex, definitely not
suited for someone looking for senior living,
but then they were young,
and that wasn't the purpose of the complex.

I asked where was the elevator,
where was the escalator,
or can't you just beam me up,
but those technologies were not in place,
so I made the trip, many, many times,
up and down, down and up,
the result, the same each time,
sore legs for an old man as I helped out,
but I was one of the lucky ones,
not having to make as many trips
carrying furniture and boxes
as the ones moving into the apartment did.

Now that all the furniture and boxes are all moved in,
and the boxes are slowly getting unpacked,
there is time to relax in the evening on their balcony
as they enjoy the view of the city,
and watching the deer come out to graze,
one of the two benefits of living on the third floor,
the view, and the exercise from their new stair climber.

A Choice of Paths

I looked out my window on the third floor
to see what businesses were around the hotel
I was staying at to get better familiarized
with my new surroundings, noticing that it appeared
the fast food restaurant next door
was the only place in town to eat at,
or at least the most popular spot as I observed
all the cars lined up in the drive-thru,
a steady line of cars headed for their
place in line from six-thirty in the morning
until ten o'clock at night, at times,
over thirty cars waiting in line.

From my on and off routine of looking out the window,
and having gotten in both of the two left-hand
turning lanes off the main drag during my visit,
I had assigned each of the lanes with a name,
with the outside lane becoming the express lane,
while the other was assigned with the name of the restaurant,
as one didn't want to get into that lane if they
had no intention of going there to eat,
knowing that their wait time would be a long one.

Yes, the traffic flow was good for their business,
but I chose a different path, a path less crowded.
To some, the wait was worthwhile,
to me, the wait was an eternity in hell.

Keeping the Yawns to a Minimum

She said I was making a lot of noise as
I sat alone in the corner, catching me
in a yawn as she walked by.

It was my first yawn of the day,
but more than likely would not be my last one.
I was aware that yawns could be contagious,

but little did I know that mine were so deafening.
I had been working on getting more sleep
to keep my yawns to a minimum,

but my progress had been slow, so I knew
I would have to work hard on keeping the noise
level of my yawns at a quieter decibel,

after all, I didn't want to disturb her again,
but if I did happen to fall asleep while I was there,
which was always a possibility,

then all I could say was watch out.
My snoring was not a thing of beauty,
where some have said that

their bark is worse than their bite,
well in my case, my snoring was definitely
worse than my yawn, something best left unheard.

Jigsaw Puzzles

The jigsaw puzzle had just been completed,
all one thousand pieces of it,
a few of the sections,
the paint worn thin from multiple uses,
and now in full display after many days,
and many hands working to fit all the pieces together.

This puzzle would remain on the table
for a few days while everyone had a chance to appreciate
the effort of those who put it all together,
then it would be taken apart in a hurried manner
and placed back into its box before the process
would start all over again with a new one.

In the meantime, maybe a few of those puzzle solvers
would attempt solving some of earth's
other mysteries before another puzzle was begun,
for I was in a maze, hopelessly lost, walking around, dazed,
where there was still hope that one of those who
participated before could help me find my way out.

Road Construction

I was driving in the right lane,
but in reality, I was in the wrong lane,
unless I wanted to wait where I was for days
as they worked on repairing the lane I was in,
but my car wasn't stockpiled with food and water
to wait it out until the construction was completed.
Instead, I switched on my turn signal,
where another driver graciously let me
over to the other lane so I could
proceed with my journey,

only to find a little while later, in different section of the city,
this time driving in the left lane,
where once again, I was in the wrong lane.
It was one of those days when it didn't seem
I could make a correct decision, with my car
seemingly wanting to follow the lanes under construction,
but I there was one good thing about the day, that
I wasn't required to make any critical decisions,
especially those affecting life and death issues,
or for that matter, even where I wanted to go for lunch.

Clown Sporting Shoes

Little did I know that a well-known sporting
apparel company made clown shoes,
but there they were, on the person right in front of me,

multi colored ones with their logo proudly
displayed on the side. Maybe the rest of his
wardrobe didn't indicate that he was

dressing up to be like a clown, but that didn't matter,
those shoes gave him away. Shoes colored
in red, cornflower blue, and white, along with a

black heal that looked a little bit like
a rubber bumper that belonged on the front
of a bumper car from the amusement park,

something that didn't match at all with the rest of the shoe,
and I had seen my share of clown shoes from my attendance
of various circuses over the years, and these definitely

fit that category, making his wardrobe unique,
but more than likely that was his intention,
as he proudly wore those shoes.

Hokey Pokey Revisited

What if the Hokey Pokey really isn't what it's all about?
  Brad Meltzer – The Escape Artist

Put your left foot in.
The process has to begin somewhere,
and the left foot is as good of a body part
as any other part of the anatomy.
I admit I never knew what it was all about,
nor even claimed that I ever knew
like some who claimed to know everything
and who were never wrong about anything.

Now put your right foot in,
and test the waters. Is it cold? Is it warm?
Oh yeah, don't forget to take your
left foot out, unless you are ready
to jump in with both feet first if you really
think you know what you are doing,
or you actually know what you are doing.

You put your head in,
but only after given it a careful thought.
You put your head out,
if you really haven't given it much thought at all.
You can skip all the other motions of the dance,
unless you are really convinced that the
Hokey Pokey really isn't what it's all about.

An Eye Exam for Mr. Magoo

Each year, I went in for my annual eye exam
and with each visit, old faithful,
the all-important eye chart was present,

the doctor asked me to remove my glasses
and read the smallest letters I could make
out on the chart, and me, knowing I could

not even make out the capital E,
the largest letter displayed at the top.
Why he still asked after reading my thick

medical chart, I did not understand?
Did he think I would develop some super
hero vision, allowing me to see through walls?

Yes, I am Mr. Magoo without my glasses,
a good reason why I wear them.
My eye sight, something not taken for granted,

always fearing I could go blind one day,
though sometimes, a blurred view of the world
was helpful from me going insane.

Handicap Parking

She parked her walker along the hallway,
next to the library door, then headed to the cafeteria
for lunch with her trusty sidekick, her cane.

I told her I didn't see any handicap parking tag
on her walker as she walked away,
and advised her she was in violation of the law,

illegally parking in that spot.
She didn't have a driver's license or a learner's
permit to wheel her walker around,

but that was the case for everyone
in the senior care facility.
The area wasn't designated for handicap parking,

then again, it wasn't marked for any kind of parking,
wondering if her walker would be towed,
issued a citation with a stern warning,

or just tell her it was okay where she parked,
but even at the age of ninety-eight,
one was never too old to learn a new trick.

Morning Workout

He walked into the YMCA,
sporting a pair of tennis shoes,
but no work-out clothes in sight,
or gym bag in hand,
sets his winter coat on the back of a chair,
pours himself a cup of coffee,
sits down, and takes a sip.
His only exercise,
walking from his car to the building,
and moving the table a few feet.

Three others join him. They talk for hours,
emptying three coffee pots,
until one finally heads to the gym,
and the two others leave.
Non-workout man puts his coat on,
but before heading back to his car,
makes another trip to the coffee pot,
getting one last cup to go.
His thirst, now fully quenched,
his mouth, well exercised.

The Hill Up Ahead

I looked out the window,
only to see a hill in the distance.
One not so steep to
prevent me from climbing it,
but what would be my purpose
in climbing to the top?
To look down
to see what was at the bottom,
only to see where I once sat?
I know where I am,
where I want to be.
Climbing the hill may be in the future,
taking the winding path,
but for now, I am in no hurry,
there are other places to visit first.

The Pacifist

With wind speeds clocking over fifty miles per hour,
nature was telling me to stay away
unless I wanted a fight.
I took her advice and stayed inside,
occasionally looking out the window
as the tree took a beating,

branches scattered over the yard,
while listening to its howls of delight.
Yes, I will wait for my turn, tomorrow,
when its anger had subsided.
Today, I am a pacifist,
waving a white flag in surrender.

A Life in Limbo

I am lost,
then found.

What is next,
I do not know?

Sometimes I care,
sometimes to do not.

I watch,
but do not see.

What is remembered,
what is forgotten?

Life goes on,
then stops.

Keep watch over me,
keep me informed.

The Ant and Its Shadow

Even the tiny ant casts a shadow
as it walks along the wooden planks
of the deck in the backyard,
the main stage for its audition.

The ant and its shadow,
walking in unison,
as if they were rehearsing a dance routine,
and now have it down pat,

ready for the cameras to roll.
Quiet on the set,
scene one, take one,
lights, camera, action.

The Paper Trail

I am not competing for a place in history.
My name was listed in the newspaper
after being born to let everyone know I had arrived,
then report cards came along,
rating me from a F to an A, pass or fail.
Did I get what I deserved?
They were posted, and I moved on
up the ladder of education.
Photographs were taken of me
as the years passed by,
growing taller and heavier,
always changing with each picture,
posing like I was a model in a fashion magazine,
except the clothes I wore were nothing fancy.
The pictures still exist, lying around,
somewhere in a photo album,
no one to look at them for years.
Again, mentioned in the newspapers,
maybe for a sporting event where I placed
in one of the top three spots,
or recognized for some award,
and finally, the paper trail will come to an end
when I pass away, and then,
just maybe, an obituary will be printed
if anyone is still around that remembers me,
and my place in history will be finalized.

My First Pet

I once had a pet crawdad.
Picked it up hiding between the rocks
in a shallow creek bed,
placed it into a bucket
filled with water from the creek,
but it did not survive long.
I guess it might have helped if I had fed it
and changed the water every so often.

I never did have another pet,
though I wouldn't have minded
having a squirrel or a rabbit as one,
but they were too fast for me to catch,
and the one pet that I did have,
I never did give it a name that I remember,
other than crawdad, and maybe
it was good I never did have another one.

Just Tell Me the Truth, What's Bothering You?

Are you in awe of stars,
the constellations at night,
the moon and the planets,
the blue skies,
and white clouds,
the sun shining down,
the world of beauty around us,
or is it something else?

Maybe it is my big smile,
my good looks,
my sense of humor,
my brain, fully loaded,
my choice in clothes,
all of the awards I have attained?
I could go on and on and on,
or have you now had enough?

Mirror Freedom

My face had gone unseen,
at least by me for several weeks
after the bathroom mirror had been removed
for a remodeling project,
and the replacement, yet to be delivered.
Were my eyebrows growing wild,
my hair all messed up,
my skin getting all wrinkly,
my nose hairs in need of a haircut?

I decided on no,
it really didn't matter what I looked like,
let the mirror be banned for life.
I look just fine,
and no one has told me otherwise.
I look as beautiful as ever,
and if unconvinced, go ahead,
just peek at my good-looking twin
in the mirror whenever it reappears.